Why I Accepted Islam

Dr A.N. May MA, Phd (Cantab)

The Islamic profession of faith - I bear witness that there is no god but God and that Muhammad is the servant and messenger of God.

Why I Accepted Islam

Dr A.N. May MA, Phd (Cantab)

BEACON BOOKS

Published in the UK by Beacon Books and Media Ltd,
60 Farringdon Road, London EC1R 3GA

ISBN 978-0-9926335-4-7

www.beaconbooks.net

A CIP catalogue record for this book is available from the British
Library.

Printed in the UK

Why I Accepted Islam

Dr A.N. May MA, Phd (Cantab)

BB
BEACON BOOKS

Published in the UK by Beacon Books and Media Ltd,
60 Farringdon Road, London EC1R 3GA

ISBN 978-0-9926335-4-7

www.beaconbooks.net

A CIP catalogue record for this book is available from the British
Library.

Printed in the UK

Contents

بسم الله الرحيم

This Book is dedicated to the oppressed
of the World.

Note: The name of God is Allah, but I use the word "God" in this book because many non-Muslims think Muslims do not believe in the same God as the Jews and Christians. Allah the God of Islam is also the God of Moses and Jesus, who are also regarded as Prophets by Muslims.

Preface to first edition

Today is a time when many people are curious about Islam. I have come to Islam, and people may be curious why any English person should do such a thing. This book is written to satisfy this curiosity. This small book is intended for people who are not Muslims, whether they are interested in becoming Muslims themselves, or simply interested in Islam. Muslims may read this book, and I hope they will find some interest here. The views expressed in this book are my own. But this is thoroughly in accordance with Islam itself, which knows no Pope or enforced orthodoxy. Equally the mistakes in this book are my own. However Islam means a great deal to me, and I hope to deepen and improve my knowledge. This book is offered simply as the work of a beginner, recently come into Islam.

Dr A.N. May MA, Phd (Cantab)
Manchester, July 1990

Preface to second edition

This personal account of becoming Muslim is an excellent introduction in quenching modern peoples thirst for spiritual meaning in the 21st century. My late husband wrote *Why I accepted Islam* 24 years ago and I pray that his reasons jolt the reader into making a well-informed opinion about Islam.

Most of the books he wrote at the time are now out of print and I wish to make them available once again. I would welcome any help, however small, in this endeavour so please contact me with your comments. I would like to thank Beacon Books for making this title available once more.

S. Haroon

Introduction

I accepted Islam on 20th June 1988, at the age of forty four, having been born in Liverpool of English and Welsh parents in 1944. I had, as I'll be showing, considered becoming a Muslim for many years previously, but in 1988 I had contacted an Islamic group in Manchester, the Dar El Ehsan, and they had actually helped me to take the final few steps. I had not found the actual step of becoming a Muslim easy. I approached a Mosque a few years earlier, but without personal friends there, had not got much further than the door.

As you can see from my age, my path to Islam was not quick or direct. As a child, I was brought up on school Christianity, which bears the same relation to real religion as do fast food burgers to real food. I had been intensely interested in Catholicism (in fiercely anti-Catholic Liverpool) at the age of 18, but had rejected it as incompatible with real commitment to help the poor and change the world into a better place. My commitment then was to Socialism and the Labour Party until I realised that this, too, had nothing to do with helping the poor and changing the world. I then became especially interested in Marxism, but never found any Marxist group or organisation that had any value, either to the poor or the World.

As this brief account makes obvious, my commitment, through all my life, has been to the poor and the downtrodden, and my aim has always been to change the World by establishing decency and kindness, and a society, a World, where human beings can grow and flourish and become marvellous people, decent and kind. My aim in this book is to tell you why I chose Islam. But that basic commitment must be kept in mind as the key to all I write here.

I went to Cambridge University to study history in October 1963, and stayed until 1969. While I was there, it is fair to say that Islam never touched me. I studied the rise of Islam for about a week in the course on the History of Medieval Europe, and all I remember of that was the commitment of the Prophet (Peace and Blessings of Allah be upon Him) to the poor. I met a few Muslims, and heard of Eid, but my Labour Party reformism lay between me and them, for the glorious Labour Party in those days was passing immigration laws and supporting Zionism. But I was never anti-Islamic, and really was completely ignorant, not realising how racist the Labour Party was, and thinking that the aim of Zionism was to save Jews from Hitler.

In the 1970s I read a little on the Prophet (Peace and Blessings of Allah be upon Him) but especially I realised how I had been deceived by the Labour Party and Zionism. This was a period of the oil crisis, and to please the rich oil powers the British press began to admit that the Palestinians were actually poor and downtrodden. I was terribly shocked to hear the truth of the events of 1948, 1956, 1967 etc. This was also a period when the complete emptiness of the Labour

Party was revealed. In 1964 I had really thought society could change. By 1974 I knew it was utterly ridiculous to think Harold Wilson would help the poor and oppressed.

I rejected these for Marxism, as I've said. I studied Marxist theory and philosophy, but the only content of Marxist activity that attracted me was anti-racist1 work. This especially meant anti-racist demonstrations, and anti-deportation demonstrations, and at one stage I was attending such an event once a week at least. Most of the deportees were, of course, Muslims, and so I began to come into contact with such groups. I was invited to attend some purely Muslim functions, and being an academic, was asked to lecture, so I found myself talking on Muhammad Iqbal, Jinnah, and the history of Pakistan etc.

The Marxism I liked was also intensely Third World centred. So I directed my academic attention nearer and nearer to the Muslim World, until in the 1980s I began lecturing on it at University. At these Muslim meetings I heard the Quran read, bought a few pamphlets, and had lots of conversations. I was invited to weddings and to people's homes. This was also a period of great upsurge in Islam, and equally great down surge in Marxism. From the mid 1980s I was seriously interested in Islam, and then in 1988 I met the Dar El Ehsan and took the final step. There are, of course, a host of reasons why I travelled this path to arrive at Islam. Some of the reasons are important. Some are trivial. And chance (which Thomas Hobbes called the hidden hand of God) played a part. In the rest of this book I will pick out some of the reasons that are especially important, and in the course of the book I will try to pick out the most important, the key reason.

I Personal Reasons

My first reason for becoming a Muslim has been personal. For many years, I have known Muslims personally, in Cambridge, London, Liverpool, Manchester and many other places. Some I met while I was an undergraduate and postgraduate student. Some I had met due to political activity. Some I just bumped into. They were mostly Pakistanis, but there were also Arabs and Iranians, and a few African Muslims. Some were students, some were working as waiters while trying to study, some were workers, some were small business people, newsagents and grocers, and some were professional people, doctors and town planners. When I really seriously considered becoming a Muslim, I met very many more Muslims very quickly. And since becoming a Muslim I have lived the life of the Muslim community.

Always from the beginning up to the present, I was very impressed with the Muslims I met. This played a big role in my accepting Islam. For any believer in anything is an ambassador for his beliefs. The Muslims, I felt, were such fine ambassadors for Islam. My comments here might strike some Muslims as strange, but I found that the personal contrast between Muslims and the non-Muslims I had known all my life was very great. Firstly the Muslims I met were clearly very sincere, deeply believing in Islam. If you wish to believe in God, and worship, it is best to do in the company of others who also believe. And if you become a Muslim, there will be no shortage of believers with whom you can mix, and share your belief. My impression is that if, in a Mosque, one hundred people are worshipping, ninety five believe absolutely in what they are doing, and the other five have some belief.

This was is marked contrast to my experience of Christianity. What I had seen was few attending church, and most believing in none of what they heard and did. People went to church for the social event, or to be seen, or for the company. Or worse, they went to do business, or to please their employers. I was more or less told that belief was for children, and old women, and not for adult men who knew the World. The content of Christianity is all interpreted away. To the Bishop of Durham and the modern theologians atheism is quite compatible with Christianity. The resurrection is a juggling trick with bones. At school the "advanced" teacher who taught religion thought the miracles of Jesus were of no value. Religious belief is dead in Europe. Increasingly it is simply a "humanistic commitment". God is merely a mankind in the abstract. They openly boast that they are worshipping Man, or human values, or whatever. This is merely amounts to vague liberalism, a veneer on non-belief.

For this reason, when the mass media insults Jesus, and films show him engaged in indecent acts, the Christians do nothing. The reason is they don't care. If religion can help the poor and oppressed, then I want to believe sincerely, and be among people who sincerely believe. This Christianity can help nobody. The outbursts of these atheistic bishops against poverty cut no ice with anyone. Rather the atheistically hypocrites to whom these protests are addressed laugh at the valueless moralizing based on "humanistic values". And the humanistic values seem elastic enough to incorporate the latest trendy attitude to abortion or whatever. The atheistic bishops run after the latest fads. (I'll consider the right-wing bishops below.) But Muslims genuinely do believe and if someone insults their Prophet (Peace and Blessings of Allah be Upon Him), that someone is in deep trouble. And the powers that be in all Muslim lands go in dread of the denunciation of their activities by the religious authorities, and do all they can to prevent open criticism. Who pays any attention to the English bishops? This deep sincerity in my Muslim friends greatly impressed me. Islam is a real presence in their lives, which they do their best to follow and grasp.

Secondly I was always impressed by what fine people the Muslims that I knew were. This Islam coincided with such fine personal features. How generous they were! How kind they were! How helpful they were! In English society I was used to calculatedness in personal relations. People were not generous, they didn't give. If they gave, it was in expectation of an exact benefit in return. They buy a round of drinks, and then sit there until all the others have bought them a drink in return. People buy, and sell friendship. If you visit them you will be offered nothing or a cup of tea and a biscuit after one hour. If you go to a public meeting, you will never get food, or if you do, you will pay for badly served and presented, second class food. In a Christian church you will go all year, and get no more than one mince pie and a glass of sherry at Christmas.

The atmosphere I was used to was the war of all against all. Then I went to Muslim meetings. Substantial meals of excellent quality were provided with no charge! In the Mosque food is provided automatically several times a week! People seemed friendly, obliging, and helpful. There was a warm atmosphere, so different to the cold hostility of English meetings. The mood was relaxed, with one feeling at home very quickly. I still note how awkward and ill at ease most English people are in each other's company. The Muslims were friendly, greeting each other, and me. Ice broke instantly. There was always a smile and everybody had such lovely manners. Above all I came to like children again. George Orwell makes many predictions in his novel Nineteen Eighty Four. One that I thought true was that by 1984 no-one would like children any more. And how I hated the children of Liverpool! Foul-mouthed, knowing, cheeky, stupid. At the sight of children I would flinch. How I dreaded the school holidays, when the little swines would be around the town all day.

Then I met Muslim families. And how charming were the children! They reminded me of the children of long ago, before modern education and childcare. You could actually talk to them without a rude answer. Their little heads were full of suitably childish ideas, not the grotesque nonsense of so many disturbed children I had met. And the kids of the Muslims looked happy and were happy. How different they are from the uncontrollable little savages I had known.

Many white people complain of having too many Muslim children in a school. Knowing Muslim children

I would never complain. They would be an asset to the school, so fine, studious and well behaved. And in the Muslim homes I went to there was a nice family atmosphere. The houses were clean and tidy, and the parents were working together. It reminded me of long ago, there didn't seem the uncertainty over roles, the bickering, and the end of family life. The parents and the children seemed to respect each other. How different this was to the scruffy homes and the disintegrated family of English society, with the uncertain values and the wretched brats. To me the best in Islam is the mass of ordinary Muslims, the Muslims masses. They know little of Islam as a theology or a philosophy. And much that they do is not Islamic. But they do lead an identifiably Islamic life, based on sincere belief, and they are an oasis in the desert of this selfish and heartless society.

Of course, there is no shortage of Muslims who do stupid things. I have had moments I would like to forget, when Muslims have been rude or objectionable. But what amazed me was they actually apologised to me, and apologized almost immediately! English people take apologising as an unforgivable sign of weakness, and I am still waiting for some people to apologise to me for bad things they did to me twenty years ago. But these Muslims actually apologised! And I could not believe how friendly they were when I became interested in Islam. I am white, and they are nearly all black, and have experienced hell from white people for hundreds of years. Yet I was instantly welcomed. And when they found I was an academic, they were keen for me to speak and write about Islam! I know exactly what would happen if a black converted to Christianity, approached an all-white church, and offered to lecture the congregation on Christianity and the nice things they said! Now you are converted, all your sins are forgiven! As a convert, you are better than us! Your prayers are twice as valuable as ours! Only really fine people could say such things. And they were honest and kept their promises. I was very impressed, as in the society I came from, because words cost nothing, they were regarded as having no value.

Thirdly, I was very impressed by how happy they were. If one was to judge a system of beliefs by how happy it made the believers, then Islam clearly comes out top. I come from English society, and the deep unhappiness of that society had always impressed me. People are so gloomy and miserable. People are afflicted with a deep sense of the pointlessness of life. People are bored with themselves, their wives and husbands, their jobs, their status in life. I think the reason for this is the selfishness and the loneliness that it causes. And the pursuit of material possessions produces an even greater sense of the emptiness and pointlessness of life. The real joy in material things can only come from giving, sharing, but above all not valuing them for themselves.

English people do none of this, the Muslims I met seemed to really enjoy material possessions, and really enjoy good food. Above all, they observed the rule of good taste, which is moderation. There are no booze-ups and blow-outs. Islam says you should not make a show of wealth, and success, because this can hurt other people. I have never met a lonely Muslim. The families are big, and despite the influence of British society, stick together. The Mosque is a place where company is always available, even if only at prayers five times a day, which always finish with the audience greeting each other and shaking hands. I have known English people with no family, and no friends at all, just a few acquaintances, and a few people one meets regularly, such as the assistants in the public library. The result is inhuman misery.

There seems to be less mental illness in the Muslim community, but this is above all due to the avoidance of alcohol. Muslims are also well known for being law-abiding. That, to me, springs from an absence of the deep restlessness there is in the non-Muslim society. A great cause of misery is the fear of death, and an obsession with the pointlessness of life that results from life's ending in nothingness. This fear of death cripples modern America, with its funeral cult and the search for the elixir of eternal life. Islam banishes all fear of death. None of the Muslims I know seem to have any of the problems with death so common in non-Muslim society.

One feature of English society is that religion as it exists seems to make people even gloomier. My memory of Christianity includes too many gloomy fanatics, half-mad with fear of hell-fire. This appears to be absent in Islam. Yet the Day of Judgement is real enough to Muslims. I feel the reason is the reasonableness of divine punishment in Islam. You will get to Paradise if you do good deeds. And God is kind and loving. And Islam believes that most human beings will end in Paradise. Some may go to hell first for a short time. A Muslim dies full of hope. In Christianity hell fire leads to madness. The Calvinists see condemnation to hell as entirely due to God's decision, and not in any way due to any good or bad deeds you've done. Many Christians feel only a small group of the elect will go to Heaven. And hell is eternal. God, to them, is more unjust than the silliest magistrate in England! But Islam says that God is more just than we could ever be. To make God less just than we are a belief I cannot accept. To God, in Islam, your good deeds, no matter how slight, outshine your bad deeds, no matter how bad.

God creates man to inherit the Universe, and God does not create any man or woman in vain. To me Christianity of all kinds was gloomy. Catholics complain of being in the grip of guilt. And I have usually felt a cold atmosphere in Christian churches. But the joy of the believers in Islam is tremendous. How they all enjoy praying! I was surprised also to find how much they enjoy fasting! And Hajj! Meetings to remember God are called Zikr, and these are the highlight of the week for the believers. This happiness is very important to me. I feel that I too can find happiness in Islam. And a real, genuine happiness. I always felt, when I heard the hymns "What a friend we have in Jesus" and "Happy Day", that if your only friend was Jesus, you would never have a happy minute, to judge by the people singing the hymns, and no-one else except Jesus would talk to you, never mind love you.

One thing that used to depress me in Christianity was the elitism, and class snobbery. The bishops and priests are way above the human beings in the audience. The church is usually a little clique of upper-class people, who cut the poor down to size, and dominate everything. In Cambridge the class snobbery and elitism around Christianity utterly revolted me. The Christians seemed very keen to dominate all the good jobs, and persecute non-believers. The followers of Christ, who loved the poor, are all public schoolboys with pots of money. The ordinary worker or housewife is quite openly despised and laughed at, in the way the English ruling classes reduce the oppressed to comic figures. Part of the happiness of Islam is the democracy. There are no priests but knowledgeable people. There is no elitism. There are no pews reserved for the squire and his lady. There are no pews. All sit on the floor in the Mosque. All snobbery is banned in Islam. I am the equal of any Saudi Arabian Monarch, when I am in the Mosque.

There is no Pope, or state church in Islam. And the democracy affects the believers. There is no inhibition in the Mosque. I have seen the most ordinary people shout out questions and objections to the most important people. Part of the happiness in Islam is the warm spontaneity of the people. The English are made, by the ruling class, to feel shy and embarrassed, ill at ease, creeping with inferiority. The Americans are much more at ease and friendly with strangers. But in Islam everyone is spontaneous, saying hello and shaking hands as soon as you meet. They do not stand on ceremony, but look, and feel, at home and relaxed. This is the World, the Home that God made for us, so why should we not feel at home and relaxed? At the same time the good manners of the Muslims prevent them from being cheeky and rude. English people I have met can be either servile, or cheeky, never treating the other person genuinely as an equal, but always feeling inferior or trying to be superior. In Islam our only superior is God. We are neither better nor worse than anyone. Only God will judge us, on the basis of our deeds.

The real happiness of Muslims never ceases to impress me. The fine character of Muslim people that has impressed me by no means implies that they have no faults, or no serious faults. Many I know are stupid, run after money, lose their tempers, commit crimes, backbite, and do all the things non-Muslims do. Many of them are only imperfectly Muslim. They are bowled over by Western values. They don't study Islam. They are lazy in obeying Islamic ideas. They give in to the constant stream of anti-Islamic abuse, and abandon Islam. But still I feel these Muslims are personally apart from the non-Muslims I have met. There seemed present in them a basic decency and kindness that I have often seen totally absent in non-Muslims. These personal qualities are very important. If I rejected Christianity, Socialism and Marxism, it was to be because you didn't feel the people with those beliefs were of good quality.

I came to the conclusion, before I became a Muslim, that the World could not be made a better place because the people available were such rubbish that nothing could be built with such people. The low personal quality of Cambridge Christians appalled me. The Labour Party seemed a lot of people out to get a bit of a job as a councillor or an MP. The Marxists were very various. But many were even more careerist than the Labour men. Many were completely selfish. Many never stopped arguing, bickering, attacking other people. Many were heavy drinkers, and were personally brutal and selfish. I wondered whether there was some sinister law of society that decreed that once a society became as unjust and oppressive as this is, it destroyed the chance of it being improved, by wrecking the moral character of the only people who could do the changing.

But then I found Islam. People with these good characteristics and personality could change this world. Islam clearly preserved them from the worst influence of this society. Where I live, the actual Muslims are the lowest working class, very badly paid and housed victims of racist attacks and police harassment. Alongside them live white people at the same economic level, but not of course, the victims of racism. It is noticeable how the Muslims preserve a level of dignity and self-respect and a style of life totally beyond their non-Muslim neighbours. Islam seems to give a real dignity and integrity to the oppressed. This, to me, is the true revenge of the downtrodden on their oppressors, to retain one's personal and moral integrity, and above all to enjoy life. Perhaps it is best to finish this account of my personal reasons by saying that this ability to retain the best human qualities while living at the bottom of society is an immense achievement for the wonderful Muslim people I know.

That is the personal reason for becoming a Muslim.

II Academic Reasons

My second reason for becoming a Muslim has been academic. As part of my academic duties, I have studied World History and World Politics today. This has led me to the study of Islam and the Islamic World. And I have realised how important Islam is in the World. And I have become aware of what role it has played, and what role it could play. I have never been interested in a virtue confined to a Monastery. Virtue has to be real deeds to help the oppressed. For that reason I could not be interested in a religion that led to withdrawal from the World. Piety is vital, but the aim of piety is to be pious in the World. Islam suits this desire in two ways.

Firstly in Islam the aim is good deeds. In some religious belief alone is enough, but in the Quran belief is never mentioned without mentioning good deeds. And careful study of the Quran shows that, in fact, belief is good deeds. Acts of kindness help to the poor and oppressed, feeding the hungry, kindness to parents and family, welcoming the stranger, are belief itself. With no good deeds, belief is hypocrisy. And good deeds breed belief. To strengthen belief in God, don't study theology, but help the oppressed. All the Islamic practises are meant to result in good deeds. Mysticism in Islam does not lead to a magic cathedral, away from human sight. Mysticism leads directly to changing the World by good deeds. For the aim of good deeds in Islam is to change the World. Good deeds are not private and personal. To many Christians good deeds exist aside from the main roads of life. In Islam the aim is to build the society and state of the One True God now. Paradise is not a consolation for a bad World. Paradise is created by us with our deeds in this World. In this World we plant the seeds that will be Paradise. So Paradise is built here. The world can be perfect. This World can be changed. There is no doctrine of original sin in Islam. Man can triumph over evil. Man can be perfect. There is no need for a saviour, or priesthood. And the good deeds of Islam are precisely the helping of the poor and the oppressed, and making a World where people truly can grow and flourish. Islam suits my desire to help the oppressed in a way no other religion does.

But Islam suits this in a second way. If something is right, then you must think it and do it no matter if you are alone. But it is a huge bonus to find that Islam is not just a belief trying to do what I want, but also a huge movement spread across the World. There are Muslims in almost all the countries of the World, and they form a majority in over 40 countries. Islam fell into a bad state many years ago, and still is in a bad state in many countries. But at the moment the Muslims are rising out of this bad state, and are returning to the real Islam. And above all else, there is, in Islam, a huge movement to help the oppressed and build the new society. This new movement in Islam is very wide and various. The movement is present in all the different groups and areas of Islam. The movement in some places is revolutionary, in others constitutional, and in some places acts politically, while in others it acts socially, building schools, clinics and even banks on Islamic lines. It is my belief that his huge upsurge of Islam can free the oppressed. And this is why, all over the World, people talk of Islam. Because Islam today actually plays the leading role in helping the downtrodden.

One hundred years ago, people looked to Europe for a system that would help the oppressed. The new Capitalists, with their democracy and science, promised to build the New Jerusalem. Especially in America, there was the dream that everyone could be a success.

The last hundred years has seen the failure of European and American Capitalism. The new society turned out to be full of greed, racism, crime, pornography, alcoholism, vandalism and an ugly inequality, in which the poor are hated and persecuted. And this system, carried to the non-European World, produced even worse societies. At least the elite of Europe have the high culture of Beethoven. The non-Europeans got Soho. The moral and physical degradation of a Thailand or a South Korea is beyond description. If Europe continues to dominate the World, it will hold back the arrival of a better society.

Fifty years ago, people looked to Stalin's Russia for a system that would help the oppressed. This hope was gone as soon as Stalin died. For a few years the Communist World tried to pretend it could compete with Capitalism, even if the dream of Communism was dead. Today the whole project stands in ruins. And for the non-Communist World, the legacy was a series of local wars in places like Ethiopia that inflicted huge suffering on the poor and oppressed.

Today Islam stands where Capitalism stood one hundred years ago and Communism stood fifty years ago. But there is a difference. Capitalism and Communism were both movements of European elites. The rich of Europe and America built Capitalism, and the highly sophisticated atheist intellectuals of Russia organised themselves into the Leninist Party. The masses were the object acted upon. The Islamic movement, though, is a movement of the masses alone. In the Muslim World the wealthy and educated are usually fiercely anti-Islamic. They have gone over to Capitalism and Communism. They do all they can to slander Islam. And the secret police do all they can to suppress Islam, killing the educated who are pro-Islamic. So Islam is left in the hands of the oppressed themselves. All these movements are the spontaneous action of the people who are the victims of society, whom the Capitalists and Communists sought to crush in their onward march. And the oppressed of the World are overwhelmingly Islamic. The worst injustice and oppression concentrate are in the Islamic countries.

It is my conviction that the oppressed everywhere need Islam. For example the black people in America have been shamefully treated by Christianity. Christianity has been the white man's religion. In the grip of white Christianity, the blacks will always be second class. Islam is the genuine non-European, non-Capitalist, non-Communist voice. This is what will save the World! By contrast look at Latin America, where the native Indians, and the descendants of African slaves and Spanish and Portuguese immigrants are kept in dependence on a Pope in faraway Italy, who is pro capitalist. Personally I feel it is my duty to be with the oppressed. In Britain the Muslims are the most downtrodden of all the people. With the rise of the new anti-Islamism, they may well undergo the fate the Jews experienced. I feel I should be with them.

A few years ago it used to be thought that the hope of mankind lay in the Third World. In the former colonies, there were lots of schemes to create a better society, from Nehru to Nasser to Nyerere to Allende. This didn't happen. Now a cheeky new Capitalism flaunts itself in these areas.

The only hope for the Third World is now the Islamic movements. And this must be the hope of all those who looked to the Third World. If the Islamic movements genuinely could create a model of society along Islamic lines, and the model worked, that would move the whole World. The prestige of Communism came from Stalin's ability to create economic growth and full employment in the 1930s, when all was economic collapse. Hundreds of millions became Communists. If an Iran, or Algeria, or Pakistan really solved its problems in an Islamic way, the whole of the oppressed of the World would come to Islam. At long last the terribly unjust and oppressive societies of the West and East would be moved, if their oppressed had a viable model of society to look to elsewhere. And the downtrodden masses of the USA, Asia and Latin America might see the way forward. The greatest problem of World affairs has been the passivity of the oppressed masses in Europe and America, who have stood doing nothing while their societies were unjust, and their governments attacking the Third World. An Islamic model, and the presence of Muslims in Europe and America, might move those oppressed masses.

These are dreams. But how marvellous it is to become a Muslim at a time when everywhere Islam is the one movement that can fully save the World from injustice and oppression. I truly believe that Islam is the hope of the most hopeless. And I believe Islam can succeed in creating a future for these people.

And that is the reason for accepting Islam that my academic studies have led me to.

III Political Reasons

My third reason for becoming a Muslim has been political. I wish to help the oppressed and downtrodden. And an Islamic movement is clearly rising up. But does Islam have the solutions to the problems that lie behind the oppression of the masses? If Islam is allowed to flourish, will it help the oppressed? Will Islamic politics help? It is my view that Islam contains the answer to the most severe political problems that weigh down on the oppressed. And it contains these answers not accidentally, but because of the basic beliefs of Islam. One of the worst problems in the modern World is racism. This is the belief that in man, biology is primary. We see this biological theory most obviously in theories of the superiority and inferiority of different colours of people. But it also shows itself in theories that man is what his physical inheritance makes him. Man is good or bad, clever or stupid, criminal or law abiding, because of what biology has given him as his fate. Racism is every type of biological fatalism.

Racism is so shocking because it produces self-confident, unthinking cruelty. The black is starved. He is refused jobs. He is condemned as stupid. His education is neglected. He is always suspected by the police. He is put in prison. All because of his biology, which he could never have chosen or altered. Islam's greatest political virtue is its complete rejection of racism and biological fatalism. Of course, the majority of Muslims are not white. And Muslims are all races and colours. But the rejection of racism is not merely due to that accident. It is deep in the history and philosophy of Islam. The Prophet (Peace and blessings of Allah be upon him) in his last sermon said that whites were not superior to blacks. And one of the closest companions of the Prophet was a black slave from Ethiopia, Bilal (May Allah be pleased with him). But the real reason is the Islamic conception of reality itself. There is no God but Allah, and the true value of a person is their obedience to Allah. Serving God is not just the most important thing. It is the only thing that counts. To look at a person's race is an insult to God. When we look at a person, we only look at their good deeds, their obedience to God.

And all men and women are created capable of obedience to God. There is no original sin in Islam. Man has the power always to do well. No creature of God is created to be punished. So to argue that some men are created wicked is to accuse God of a terrible crime. All men and women can become wonderful people. All are equally capable of goodness. Central to racism and biological fatalism are the ideas of Darwin, the belief that the World is a place ruthless competition and savagery. To these people, the world is unreasonable, vicious and mad. Man must be a wolf to man. But to Islam Allah is merciful and compassionate. The World is a kind and loving place. It is Man's home. The World is not a mad and bad place. What makes it bad is Man's failure to worship God. Darwinism is an insult to, and a slander against God. Modern social and biological science fully confirms Islam.

The causes of crime are not race, but a bad and selfish society. Men are not born with a given level of intelligence or ability. If the World is a war of wolves, this is due to Capitalism, which sets all against all in ruthless competition. I have no doubt that Islam is absolutely correct in rejecting racism and biological fatalism.

Other religions, however, are polluted with racism. Hindu castes are identical in their effects and implications to the worst racism. One is born into a level of goodness. Judaism is infected today with Zionism, and a cult of racial exclusiveness. Christianity such as I've seen is deeply stained with racism. It is the white man's religion. In the case of Hinduism, there appear to be racial assumptions in the basic philosophy. In Judaism there should be no racism, but the Zionists build on the idea of the Jewish nation to copy racial theories. In Christianity there should be no racism. But I think that the theological doctrines of original sin, and the idea of God's elect and the belief in complete fatalism found in Calvinism, inclines Christianity to accept racism. Islam, of course, holds that the original prophets of Judaism and Christianity were completely Muslim. So it is a total disgrace to those religions if any racism has crept in. Only Islam has kept faith with the prophets.

I deeply feel that one should realise the full horror of Zionist and Christian racism: the endless persecution of the Palestinians; the acceptance by the churches of the black slave trade; the acceptance of Apartheid as God-given by some Christian churches; the inactivity of so many Christians and so many Churches at the time of Hitler's murders. As a white man, I feel Islam is the best, if not the only way to forget racism, and put it behind you. Islam is the religion for all races. But also Islam is centred, historically, outside the white race. And white people have such a role to play in Islam, building the true brotherhood and sisterhood with the black people who will be beside them in the Mosques. Islam is thus the way for white people to forget racism.

I have spoken of how happy I feel in the Muslim community. This forgetting of racism is a great source of joy to me. I must not just mention the racism of religion. I found Labour Party racism one of the worst features of reformism. And the communists clearly cared little for non-whites. The complete silence over the millions of dead and refugees in Afghanistan showed me the true racism of people who claimed to be Marxist proletarian internationalists.

One of the worst problems in the modern World is nationalism. This is very closely related to racism, and much more of what I've said before applies here. But whereas few people worship a race, nearly everybody worships their own nation. Most people will kill for nation. And the nation is a tremendous hindrance to the solution of human problems. Most politicians are only concerned for their voters or party members, and foreigners can never vote for you, or hold the party card.

There are plenty of people who claim to be internationalists. But it seems a weak and insipid commitment, alongside the flag-waving crowds. The vague humanism of the brotherhood of man seems to convince nobody. Islam absolutely rejects the nation, and for the deepest of reasons.

All men are directly under God, and the only thing that matters is obedience to God, which is goodness. So in Islam the only unit is the unit of all the good people. Islam is the movement of the good people, which is called the Ummah. And the aim is for the movement of good people to grow and grow and take in all people everywhere. And so good people everywhere are fellow-citizens in Islam. No national barrier can stand in the way of goodness, of obedience to God. Islam is thus in its bones a movement that crosses frontiers. And I, in Britain, am the brother of any good person anywhere. Muslims call each other brother and sister. Now the real point is that Muslims mean it.

There are no national churches in Islam, no state churches. Sects of any kind are disliked and condemned. The Muslims of, say, Iran do not hesitate to reach out to the Muslims of Saudi Arabia, and vice versa. And there is an annual gathering of Muslims from every nation. It is the Hajj in Makkah.

One common confusion is that Islam is Arab nationalism. Many of the regimes and movements in the Arab World became infected with European nationalism, but this nationalism is modern and atheistic. The Prophet (Peace and blessings of Allah be upon him) was an Arab, but he said that Arab and non-Arab were equal. The Prophet (Peace and blessings of Allah be upon him) was sent to the Arabs, and the Quran is in Arabic, and can never be adequately understood in any other language. But, to me, God chose the Arabs because they were the poorest of the poor, the dwellers in a vast hostile wilderness. It was their humble position that set them aside, and certainly no racial superiority.

One of the worst problems in the modern World in the oppression of religions. And this is the worst of all oppressions, for man is denied the chance to seek after God, and the most sacred beliefs are polluted with the filth of sectarian hate. This is oppression which attempts to reach into men's souls. And beyond the grave. And it is the most oppressive because it can achieve the real goal of all oppressors, which is to morally degrade the victim. The victim becomes robbed of his moral and spiritual integrity, of his soul. The filthiness of sectarianism can be seen in Northern Ireland, where the level of hatred is beyond belief.

Religious persecution, though, in the modern World is not rooted in religious belief or lack of it. Rather it is the result of the use of religion for imperialist and colonialist ends. The great white imperialist powers all used religion as their flag. The Spaniards used Catholicism in Latin America, the French and British used Christianity in Africa and Asia, and the Russian Empire of the Tsar used Russian Orthodoxy on their borders to justify the attacks on a host of countries. Muhammad Iqbal, the greatest thinker of modern India, wrote that the cause of atheism was the misbehaviour of Christians. And the use of religion for imperialism was the worst example of this misbehaviour. Who can fail to reject religion if Christ is made to preach the extermination of the American Indians, or the mass murders of the Tsar?

The Marxist atheist feels morally purer for his rejection of religion. And in reply to Communism religion was made to preach the goodness of Capitalism, the lightness of inequality, the virtue of wickedness. In modern America the poor are left out of the Bible! So in the World we have persecutor Christianity, and in reply persecutor Atheism. Zionism rides along on the back of Christianity. There are, of course, persecuted Catholics in Northern Ireland, persecuted by Protestants. Typically the Pope ignores their sufferings, and lectures them on the need to accept Britain. The result is the turn of Sinn Fein to Marxism.

One result of this history of oppression is that religious oppression almost exclusively means the oppression of Islam. But more than that, Islam is everywhere an oppressed religion. This is due to the rooting of Imperialism in Western Capitalism, which Islam, as we'll see, rejects. Rejecting Western Capitalism, Islam could never develop the imperialism which springs from Capitalism. So Islam was the victim and target of the imperialists. The French targeted African Islam, the British aimed at Arab and Indian Islam, and the Russians the Islam of its southern borders.

Islam is thus the religion of the victims of imperialism. Also because the Muslim World is ruled by pro-imperialist groups, Islam is a persecuted religion in countries which are one hundred per cent Muslim. In Britain the BBC turns out continuous rubbishy Christian programmes and the blasphemy laws ensure respect. In an Egypt, Tunisia, or Jordan openly anti-Islamic persons will scoff at Islam on the TV! Islam is also, of course, persecuted directly in the non-Muslim World; The Bulgarians force Muslims to take different names. The Russians until recently kept Mosques closed. In Britain any Christian group can have separate schools. In Northern Ireland the hated Catholics are allowed separate schools. Muslims have no separate school, one irony results. As I've said, no-one really believes in Christianity any more. Mass atheism is the reality. So the Christians are free, but don't do anything with their freedom. They don't wish to build a Christian society any more. Christians oppress, when they don't wish to convert anyone to anything worth the effort. The Christian schools are really secular schools in all things. But the Muslims do wish to do things. Given freedom, they would build a Muslim society. Given schools, those schools would have a unique religious atmosphere.

Thus it is ninety-five percent true to say that the only people who wish to be religious in the World today are persecuted, and stopped from being religious. Very simply, then, religious freedom today means freedom for Islam. All people who genuinely are religious should fight for the right of the people who genuinely believe to worship God. My reason for becoming a Muslim is partly the desire to be with the genuine believers, as I've said. But anyone who loves the worship of God, and spirituality, should support Islam, no matter what their own belief. A man may be an atheist, unable to accept religion for philosophical or scientific reasons. He may still see a value in religion for those who do not share his doubts. He should support Islam's freedom. To value religious freedom means to support Islam. My experience with genuinely religious people is that they are not merely tolerant, but take a great delight in people of other beliefs who genuinely believe.

How fascinating to compare notes! How confirming of my belief is someone's belief in something slightly different, but also basically or even slightly, the same. Imam Ghazzali, the greatest Muslim after Prophet Muhammad (Peace and blessings of Allah be upon him) put sectarianism down to the selfishness of people. These people don't love God, they love themselves. A genuine believer loves God so much that he stresses the things he agrees about with others, not the things he disagrees with. Islam holds, also, that there can be no compulsion in religion. Islam's "conquests" were made in self-defence, against powerful neighbours who were determined to get rid of Islam. Islam also holds that all religions, if rightly understood, are the same as Islam. Judaism's prophets are prophets for Muslims too, and the Torah and Psalms are holy books for them. Christ is a prophet of Islam. Sincere Muslims, consequently, are not in any way hostile to these religions.

For all these reasons I feel that a toleration of Islam would be an enormous boost for religion, and religions. Religious freedom for Islam would hugely enrich the religious atmosphere of the whole World. Incidentally, the oppression of Islam isn't working. Islam is everywhere up surging. The endless stream of lies and hate has no effect, or the opposite effect to that intended. Muslims have heard all the lies before.

Let us not forget the real reason why Islam is persecuted. The persecution was, and is to some extent mere expediency, divide-and-rule tactics. But Islam is really persecuted because it is the total enemy of imperialism. Islam hates racism, nationalism, greed and all that imperialism stands for. Christianity is on the BBC hundreds of times a week for the opposite reason. Islam is hated by all oppressors, and always will be. That, of course, is why I choose Islam.

One very pronounced feature of the modern World is that all reaction is anti-Islamic. The West has a history of oppression, but there are some beliefs that take this oppression to its ultimate nightmarish extremes. These beliefs are usually called fascist or Nazi. These fascists or Nazis are always anti-Islamic. Le Pen, in France, leads one of the most successful fascist movements in Europe. But he is less a racist than he is sectarian, anti-Islamic. His hated enemy is the Muslim population of France. His fear, he says, is that France will become an Islamic republic. Personally he took part in the French war in Algeria which killed millions of Muslims. In Germany the Nazis above all hate Turks. They hunt them on the Berlin underground. In Britain, the worst racism of the National Front is against Pakistanis.

Some of these Nazis have friends in the Muslim World. It seems clear that many governments there supply them with help. But these regimes and people are not the Muslims. They are the anti-Islamic Westernized elites, who have accepted the racism and fascism of Europe.

If some in the Muslim World join with anti-Islamic reaction, so do many Western liberals. Historically, extreme fascism has always tried to present itself as progressive. Anti-Semitism portrayed itself as anti-Capitalism and was taken as such, by fools. Similarly the anti-Islamists try to appeal to the liberals, and the left. They try to argue that Islam is feudal and oppressive. Because of Afghanistan, many leftists repeated this.

But it is the belief of fools. There are many reasons why the Le Pen's are anti-Muslim. We've already seen the role of imperialism. But there are other reasons. Islam is a self-confident belief entirely outside the white race. As such it rivals fascism as no other belief does. The history of Marxist movements has shown all too often that Marxism is a belief of the oppressed second and the white man first. The behaviour of the French Communist Party over Algeria, when it told the Algerians to submit to France, is a case in point.

The key reason, though, for fascism's hostility to Islam is that in the West the Muslims are the very bottom of society. They are the most exploited, the most downtrodden. The Bengalis in the East End of London work for nothing in sweat shops. The Muslims form ghettos in Bradford, Paris, and Marseilles. In the Soviet Union the masses of Muslims in Azerbaijan and the rest of Soviet Central Asia live worse than any other group of Soviet citizens. These Muslims in Britain, France or Russia etc can be allowed no freedom. They must be kept down in complete terror. They must not even be allowed to feel at home in Britain and France, but must always be about to be deported. In Russia they are denied their culture in the lands that have been theirs for centuries. Against these Muslims at the bottom of society the West uses the same lynch law and mob terror that was used against American blacks. How often have I read of Mosques being burnt, of pigs' heads being thrown into a Mosque, of crowds leaving the Mosque being attacked after prayers by men dressed as the Ku Klux Klan.

How much it is our duty to be Muslims and pro-Islamic! Western society was nearly annihilated by anti-Semitism. If anti-Islamism is allowed to grow and develop, we may well find an anti-Islamic Hitler coming to power. The liberals who add to the abuse are making a stick that will one day be used on them. Anti-Islamism is the liberation of the fools, the anti-feudalism of fools. Equally it is vital, for the health of Western society, to show that Islam is good, progressive and deserving of toleration in the West and in the Third World. In the new age rising after the collapse of communism, a new Cold war against Islam may begin. This will spoil the new peace and prosperity with the threat of endless war and tensions. The freedom of Islam is really vital to the World. It is however, extremely easy to show that Islam really is progressive, and progressive in the sense that the term is understood in the West. I have already shown Islam's anti-racism, anti-nationalism and anti-imperialism. Islam has a host of other positive political aspects.

Islam is often presented as a type of feudalism. Many regimes, also, in Muslim countries, have feudal features. But Islam is in its essence totally opposed to feudalism. The feudal features arose because Islam spread in feudal societies, which kept many of their feudal features. But all of feudalism is anti-Islamic. There can be no feudal aristocracy because Islam rejects the whole idea of aristocrats. All men are equal, and man's only master is God. And one's loyalty is only to God. To pledge fealty, lifelong loyalty to a man and his heirs would be to make a little god out of a man. Fealty is to God alone. Also there is no priesthood in Islam, and so no Pope. As a result there is a freedom to differ In Islam unknown in Christianity. Now where would Medieval Feudalism be with no Pope, priest, or lord? The rigid estates and castes of Medieval Europe are closer to Hinduism, and not Islam.

Islam is also totally anti-capitalist. This anti-capitalism goes deep into Islam. Capitalism is systematic self-worship, in which the goal is benefit to the self, and ultimately pleasure of an infinite amount and variety. The motivation of capitalism, its engine, is the pursuit of profit, which is selfish gain. To get the profit other selves are exploited, systematically. One self is dominated by another self in the web of relations called the World market. All of Capitalist politics is the rights of the self to be selfish. The self can do whatever it likes, as long as the other selves accept the contracts involved. This unlimited right of selfishness is called "freedom". "Freedom" is the chance to be totally selfish, and pursue benefit and pleasure. All of Capitalist ideology is this self-worship, whether it is Thatcherism, or the Existentialists, or the antics of "artists" who indulge their fantasies, and exhibit themselves to public gaze.

In Islam only God is worshipped. The one thing you do not worship is yourself. You teach yourself not to follow your selfish desires, and not to seek benefit and pleasure. You seek to be kind and decent to other selves, and never to mistreat them, for they are all God's creatures, and equal to you. In this way all of Capitalism falls. Most of the pleasures of Capitalism are forbidden, such as alcohol and pornography. "Riba" is forbidden. This is usually translated as interest on money, but it also has the wider meaning of exploitation. Islam also forbids unemployment, which is necessary for the Capitalist system to frighten the worker into obeying the orders of his employer. Islam insists that everyone has the right to eat. Islam also says that all must work, and so forbids the existence of a class of rich parasites. Islam forbids greed, and says you must control your desires. Islam commands kindness to the poor. Islam also allows the market, but forbids all cheating in trade. A trader must never deceive his customers, and must tell them the true value of his goods for sale, and take back without question any faulty goods. In Islam we give up selfishness to serve God and to make the World a fit place for God's creatures.

Islam does recognise property based on your own work, and, as I've said, trade and commerce. So Islam is not Communism. There is also no place in Islam for State worship, worship of the political party, and worship of the working class. The Ummah, the Mosque and the devout Muslim replace these key elements in Communism. But Islam does have the love of the poor, and of serving the people, and an emphasis on plain living and hard struggle found in Mao Tsetung. The "goulash communism" of the Soviets, with its pursuit of an endlessly escalating level of benefit and pleasure, is as alien to Islam as the Capitalist efforts to achieve the same thing.

The West makes much of democracy. That democracy is the political counterpart of "freedom". The selfish selves agree to tolerate each other and accept the majority verdict. Islam already contains democracy, for it says that we should regulate our affairs by consultation. But Western Democracy becomes collective selfishness. There are no limits to the sovereignty of the combined selves. Anything can be made legal, or illegal. And so democracy becomes a vehicle for selfishness. Also, despite all the talk of equality, the rich few run the democratic governments. Their wealth and education, and skills, and their control of the media and the economy enable them to win any election, or overpower any elected government. The poor and exploited have equality, but only equality in theory, in the textbook, and not in practice. How can there be equality between exploiter and exploited, between rich and poor? Democracy is the instrument that blesses, in the name of "freedom", the selfish schemes of the enormously wealthy and powerful few.

In Islam the democracy must be real, not just on paper. There must not be the huge inequalities giving the few the right to dominate the many. In the consultation, the voices of all must be heard, not just the voices of those who dominate the media. And there are limits to what the government can do. Man must be ruled by the law of God. Thus there is no concept of unrestricted sovereignty, of total power over anything in Islam. The law of God is clear and known, and it cannot be changed.

Islam thus completely rejects any totalitarianism, and any dictatorship, unelected or elected. The only guarantee of a real human freedom and dignity is obedience to the law of God, and so the commitment of a huge mass of the population to learning and knowing and understanding the Holy Book of Islam, the Quran. What is needed is a mass of people with the fine human qualities Islam can give. Western democracy promises. Only the reality of a majority of sincere and devout persons in the population can deliver. Islam replaces the "freedom" of the West with real freedom.

This Islamic economics and politics are coming into existence at this moment in many parts of the World. There have been many failures and disasters. Islam will only triumph if it can truly live up to the essence of Islam as I've described it. But I feel that this Islamic politics and economics can produce a society that really frees the oppressed, establishing a decent and kind society with no racism, no nationalism, no religious oppression, no economic exploitation, and no tyranny, elected or unelected.

And that is my political reason for choosing Islam.

IV Moral Reasons

My fourth reason for becoming a Muslim has been moral. I like the way Islam says we must live our lives, and what our conduct should be. Now of course I have already in this book described many features of Islamic morality, from the anti-racism to the conduct of traders. This morality also played a big role for me personally in moulding my view of Islam. At Cambridge I was appalled to see how the undergraduates often treated their parents, and were treated by them. I remember how struck I was, when once a passage from the Quran recommending kindness to parents, was translated for my benefit.

I was especially attracted by the rejection by Islam of alcohol in all its forms. In Britain, nine out often social problems are rooted in alcohol. Ninety per cent of violent crimes are committed by drunken men. Much theft is to buy drink. Most vandalism is something drunks do late at night. One quarter of hospital beds are filled in this country by people suffering because they drink too much alcohol. But more importantly I have learned that people drink and become alcoholics because of oppression. Men drink due to having to work excessive hours. People drink because of the burden of worry due to unemployment, bad housing and ill health. The lazy oppressor, who is determined to never work, drinks to kill time. Also the breweries do all they can to sell drink so as to make huge profits. But people drink above all due to ignorance, due to having no other way of passing the time because of brainlessness.

Alcohol is inseparable from an unjust and oppressive society, and when Islam simply rejects it, it works wonders for the oppressed. The poor Muslims cope so much better than their poor non-Muslim neighbours partly because they avoid drink. It gives them that extra dignity. The rejection of drink is the rejection of oppression.

There are, of course, many details of Islamic morality that I could describe. But what particularly attract me are not just the details, but certain features of Islamic morality in general. One feature I especially value is the seriousness with which life is treated. To many people today, life is a joke, too unimportant to bother about. Life becomes one long laugh. The aim is to be constantly surrounded by empty amusements. One spends an evening sitting in front of the TV, while a lot of fools pass the time in providing something called entertainment - rubbish quiz games, endless situation comedies, soap operas, and football matches. Relaxation has its place. Islam knows its festivals. But this endless pursuit of trivia is more than these. The real World of suffering and oppression is forgotten. The uncomfortable reality of life is just swept under the carpet of triviality.

The mass of people in the West can tolerate a World of eight hundred million starving people because they are sunk in an endless round of parties, holidays and golf. To them, even a murder or similar tragedy is just a real-life entertainment. How eagerly they watch the film of the air disaster or the riot! To Islam this triviality is totally alien. Life is serious business. The Muslim should fill his whole day with only two things, says Imam Ghazzali. They are providing for this life, and providing for the life after death.

All else is forbidden. You should remember God at all times and in all places. Also the Prophet (Peace and Blessings of Allah be upon Him) said that if you knew what the Day of Judgement was like, you would laugh less than you do. Muslims are happy people. They know God is loving and compassionate. But their happiness is mature, thoughtful happiness. And the happiness coexists with seriousness. Thus Islam prescribes what food may be eaten, and what may not be eaten. But the lesson is above all that food is serious business. When we sit down to eat, we always remember God, if only by saying God's name when taking the first sip or bite. Food is not a game, too many are without it. We take eating seriously.

A second feature of Islamic morality is how it relates to happiness. There are many different views of what happiness is. To some happiness is success, passing exams and becoming important. To other happiness is huge wealth. In the West today happiness is above all seen as pleasure, an endless round of eating, drinking, entertainments and especially sexual activity. In Islam happiness in none of those things. Happiness is very simply moral goodness. Goodness is the obeying of God's law. But that doesn't merely make you happy. Such obedience is happiness. So morality is not only serious, it is also happy. The Muslims have their happiness because they are trying to be good people, and not because of endless trivial amusements. But especially, the good deeds of Islam are the lifting up of the oppressed.

The true happiness in life is thus precisely the commitment to the poor and the downtrodden that is so vital to me, and so vital to Islam. In most other moralities, as we've seen, there is no real commitment to the oppressed. But there are moral codes which, though different to Islam, have the same commitment to the oppressed. When we look at these, though, we see some big differences to Islam's morality. I am thinking, of course, of Marxism. Christianity is too polluted with imperialism and racism to be worthy of concern. The right-wing bishops dominate the churches, and tell the poor to do nothing, to submit to oppression. But the Marxists tell the poor to never accept their poverty. Marxist morality also has many fine features. There is a total commitment to opposing racism and the oppressive nationalism of colonialism and imperialism. There is a denunciation of class oppression and exploitation. The ideal of communism is very inspiring. Ultimately communism is the readiness to die for the oppressed. And yet it all failed.

In my opinion the reason for failure is the key difference between Islamic morality and Marxist morality. And it is a very simple problem. A Communist society is very admirable morally. It brings direct benefit to the oppressed. For example the unemployed directly benefit in a society where it is illegal to be unemployed. But why should I obey Marxist morality if I am not directly benefiting? Why should anyone who has a comfortable life, bother to fight for the oppressed? Why should I fight if I can have a prosperous life in the future? But above all, why should anyone die for the oppressed? I may be living a poor life, even a life of terrible poverty. But if death is the end, will not life as a slave be better than eternal death? And if my life is remotely acceptable, to die for other people who are poor is lunatic (If death is the end).

Is it not better to settle for the soft option? Become a reformist, and try to get a nice soft job. Or join the oppressors, and have a marvellous life as a traitor to the cause. And if Communism does triumph, turn the triumph to a selfish gain! Instead of being a revolutionary cadre, become a well-fed bureaucrat in a nice job, and then finally become just like any other Capitalist. So, in brief: Communism is a readiness to die for the poor; but how can an atheist die for the poor? To abuse Marxism it was usual to say that it was a religion. They thought it could not be really scientific to wish to help the oppressed. The problem with Marxism was, though, precisely that it was not a religion. Marx thought religion was a support for the Capitalists. So, to fight Capitalism you had to be an atheist. Marx was, of course, correct in relation to the religion he knew, which was Christianity. The problem was, though, that no real struggle against oppression could survive which was not religious. The early Marxists retained, unquestioningly, that commitment to die if necessary for the poor. But once the Lenins and the Maos (and the Stalins) were gone, the Marxists decayed. And nothing in the ideology could pull it back from collapse.

Soon the Communists became simply the selfish pleasure-seekers that the Capitalists always were. They became hypnotised by the American way of life. Plain living and hard struggle were no more. So Communism simply collapsed for lack of Communists. The old slogans became so much official hypocrisy. What is needed, then, is a total commitment to the oppressed that will not flinch in the face of death. A new belief is needed that will justify dying for the poor.

Islam is such a belief. God will compel Man finally to set up a real Paradise, where oppression is no more. No one who is a Muslim need fear for one second that he is giving up something by accepting the pain and suffering and death that comes from fighting the oppressor. Muslims, of course, lose heart. They become corrupted and selfish. The history of Islam is a series of failures of this kind. But the point there is the word "series". When a wave of Muslims has become corrupt, there is within Islam the moral energy to revive again the struggle for the oppressed.

Islamic morality has an ingredient that Marxist morality lacks. Islamic morality is not only admirable, and a benefit to the oppressed. There is a real reason for every person, no matter how rich and privileged, to obey it. That is the key difference. Funnily enough one of my first questions to Marxists at Cambridge was how the struggle had any point if death was the end. That question was the key to the failure of Marxism. Islam's complete commitment to the Day of Judgement makes Islam absolutely the right belief for anyone who really wishes to help the oppressed.

Islam's commitment to the Day of Judgement is also unique among religions. The Quran makes clear that other religions always insist that the Day of Judgement doesn't apply to them. The Quran points to Judaism's idea of the exemption of Jews from judgement, and to the Christian idea that Christ shields all believers from the perils of that day. It is not only Marxism that fails on this point.

There is also a second way Islamic morality differs from Marxism's. Marxism has fine principles, but it leaves the question at generalities. There is a lack of detail. The same is true of Christianity. We are left with the command to love. But life consists of details. Most of the time we are doing trivial little things, like eating, washing, dressing, sleeping, walking, meeting friends etc. Islam has its general principles. But these principles have also been worked into a detailed code for everyday life. In this it is similar to certain types of Judaism. Now this detailed code means that we can carry our politics and morality into the trivial things of which life consists. So we can lead a life of total morality and total politics. A few examples will illustrate.

All men are brothers, so when you meet you must say "peace be upon you" (Assalamu Alaikum). A Muslim must have no pride, feeling better than others. Only God is man's superior, not man. So when you walk, you must not walk arrogantly. Your dress must be smart, but plain and simple. When you sit, you sit directly on the floor, as befits a servant of God. A Muslim always remembers God, so when you wash you say God's name. A Muslim models himself on the Prophet (Peace and Blessings of Allah be upon him), so a Muslim should carry a walking-stick, as did the Prophet (Peace and Blessings of Allah be upon him). You must face Makkah when you pray, but also when you sleep, and when you are buried. When you wake you must say God's name.

These details seem excessive. But they are the solution to a problem of modern life. In the last thirty years there has been a largely successful attempt to annihilate the culture of ordinary life. Manners have gone. Children are not taught them. So children never stand up on a bus to let women sit down, for example. All elegance has gone out of dress. Prosperous people dress like tramps, in T-shirts and scruffy jeans. The "decolouration" has been the work largely of the Freudian counterculture of the 1960s. Culture, they believe, is repression of subconscious impulses.

So culture must be annihilated and replaced by unrestrained annihilated. As a result the leaders of art and culture are savage philistines. Rushdie adheres to this artistic philosophy. This "decolouration" has gone so far that all the niceness has gone out of life. One walks down dirty and untidy streets, passing men and women dressed as tramps, to sit in filthy homes, and never to hear a kind or welcoming word.

Islam offers the only way to "recalculate" life. Part of the rebellion against culture was the recognition that much culture was oppressive. There was the culture of petty snobbery that I met at Cambridge with its intellectual one-upmanship and deliberate mocking of people who work for a living. Especially revolting is the wine snobbery, with swanking about drinking wine from a certain country and year. To reject such "culture" is a step forward. Such "culture" was philistinism. But Islam offers enculturation on the basis of a total commitment to the oppressed. The life Islam offers is the most elevated principles in living detailed form.

This collapse of culture is part of a wider problem. In the Nineteenth Century the philosopher said God was dead. In the Twentieth Century the philosopher says Man is dead. The central concept of Western thinking is that of the individual. All of society is sacrificed to make way for this individual, which is the self. In the Renaissance and later the greatest achievements were the great individuals, the Leonardo's and Beethoven's. But then the dream went sour. The totally selfish society ends by destroying the individual. The typical person of today is the tool of the state and the media. He is the organisation man, the soulless official. In place of the individual we have above all the consumer. We have a herd mentality. There is the complete collapse of integrity, standards, decency and conscience. Life degenerates into an endless round of trivia. Modern life is as absurd as it is cruel. There are no individuals left, and the critics of Western society are as bad as the society. Nowhere is there such lack of conscience and herd mentality as there is among the radicals, and the left. Everyone is conforming to the tyranny of narrow-minded public opinion. And this life is absolutely pointless. Human dignity is replaced by the manipulation of advertising and the hysterical popular press. Above all there is an utter lawlessness to modern life. It is not that people are wicked, or have bad standards, but rather that there exists a deep moral anarchy. The collapse of human life goes well beyond the end of culture. Civilised society is peopled by savages.

If people worship anything, it is power. All that matters is success. Only victory counts. Break every law of God and Man as long as you win! This brings me to the key to modern life. It was not just Marxism that abolished belief in life after death. Throughout the West, as George Orwell wrote, the biggest event of the modern age has been the end of belief in life beyond the grave. Today, for example, it is common to see cartoons joking about the punishments of Hell. No one who believed in life after death could for one second make such jokes. The belief that death is the end has produced a variety of responses, all of which account for the restlessness of modern man. If death is the end, then life is clearly absolutely pointless. So one response is to trivialise life. Try to kill the sense of meaninglessness by watching the antics of the clowns. A second response is to just try to forget, to achieve the death in life that conies from alcohol or drugs. A third response is to make life the pursuit of delights, and especially of sexual delights.

A fourth response is to regard life as a cruel joke. Man is, by virtue of being born, inevitably the victim of a cruel and malignant fate. This is the idea of Schopenhauer. Life is irredeemably tragic; man is born to pointlessness, and has the illusion that life has point. But the more he tries, the more pointless life is. All our efforts are laughed to scorn. From the philosophy of Schopenhauer two conclusions have been drawn. The first is that mankind should quietly fade away. This arrives at Buddhism. Suffering is eternal and cannot be ended. The poor and oppressed cannot be helped. The poor are always with us. The cause of the suffering is precisely the craving for a better World, for pleasure and permanence. So the solution is to renounce the World. Give up your passion, frustration and desires. Do this by self-denial and Buddhist meditation. The World is not to be changed, it is to be renounced. This Buddhism is immensely popular. It converges with the pursuit of pleasure and drugs, because it agrees with such pursuit that the oppressed can be ignored. To them to try to help the poor is the Marxist fallacy, a fallacy because death is the end. The second conclusion from the philosophy is the one drawn by Hitler. If life is a pointless and cruel joke, then the best thing to be is a pointless and cruel joker. Go down to destruction, but raise a huge protest against this by smashing up the World before you go!

The fifth response to the belief that death is the end is a variety of strategies aiming at achieving immortality. Some people have fantasies about living for three hundred years, and so go in for a variety of cures, foods and exercise. They usually drop dead at fifty! In America there is a whole death industry, with coffins fitted with stereos, and videos of the deceased. But these strategies of immortality usually do no more than make the fear of death worse.

The sixth response was the one Orwell analyzed. It was the worship of power. If death is the end, identify totally with some large group outside yourself, such as the white race, the proletariat, Russia, Zionism, Britain, the Catholic Church, "Women", your own nation etc This larger group will survive your death. Then worship this group. Make a god out of it. Completely merge yourself with it. And then you become immortal, for when you are dead this group which you are totally a part of will survive. This craving for "group worship" is the real secret to much that goes on. Because the group is the ticket to eternity, its interests must be promoted at all times. It must be defended at all costs. It must have complete justice on its side in every situation and at every moment. These racists, nationalists, Zionists, or whatever, are really weeping in the dark of heir fear of death.

The worship of power links with the seventh response. If no God exists, every crime is justified. But more important, the more crimes you commit, the better. Real success is triumphing over other people, over the oppressed. If you want real power, you must make people suffer. These racists, etc, really worship their group when it is cruel. Successful cruelty becomes the true immortality. The last response to the finality of death is the cheapening and trivialising of human life and death. The aim is selfish pleasure now. If people have to die for my pleasure, so be it! The obvious example here is abortion. To take the life of a totally innocent unborn baby is a frightful act. It is justified because the baby would be a nuisance, which would make "life" "unpleasant". And the killing of the unborn becomes a disgusting little minor operation, like an enemy.

Now the obvious point from all this is that the belief that death is final is a catastrophe for all, and especially for the oppressed. It is the major reason for the death of Man. Islam has the solution. It is a religion in which people really believe, which holds that the Day of Judgement and Paradise are absolutely real. The point is very simple. A few more decades of belief that death is the end, and mankind will be finished completely. There are no depths to which we cannot sink. Islamic morality is absolutely vital to the life of mankind. Islam says that because of death there is no reason to feel pointless, or to try to forget, or to just pursue delights, or to be a Buddhist, or a Hitler, or to seek power and cruelty. Rather the reverse, because you will die you must take life seriously, be alert, conscious, kind and decent.

Man need not die in the Twentieth Century. That is my moral reason for choosing Islam.

V Islam Alone Remains

My fifth reason for becoming a Muslim is that Islam alone remains. All else has failed. These other beliefs and ways of life are now more than false. Life simply can no longer go on in the old ways. The complete collapse of ideologies is part of the crisis of modern man. Man is not only dead. He is lost in the midst of the debris of previous beliefs. The result is a deep spiritual crisis. I believe that Islam alone can be the way out of the crisis. All the gods have failed except God. To begin with Marxism. I have made many comments on Marxism, but these comments are not needed to produce any crisis in Marxism. As events in Russia and Eastern Europe unfold, Marxism is finished as a way of life. Hundreds of millions now know that Communism cannot be built.

But not only is revolutionary Socialism dead. Reformism is also dead. The ideas of creating a more just "post-capitalist" society died in the 1980s. Keynes, nationalisation, the Welfare State are all clearly on the way out. Capitalism cannot be reformed. Not only has Socialism failed, but the Working Class has failed. The idea that the industrial proletariat would build a better World is now laughable. They are no longer the hope of the World, but seem to be caught in the web of Capitalism completely. The liberator class reads The Sun, is racist, and just worries about the rate of interest on their mortgaged houses. Like the American working class, the European working class is the pillar of the oppressive system. They are not the solution, they are the problem.

The great hope of the future was once Science and Technology. Religion was despised because it was thought to stand in the way of the high technology society. Philosophers like Bertrand Russell and Wittgenstein tried to argue that all religious and philosophical problems could be dispensed with and ignored. To Wittgenstein they were just linguistic confusion. Divine Justice is a language muddle! The philosophical result of the worship of science was deep gloom. To Russell the basis for thinking had to be complete despair. But nowadays this making of science into a god, as well as being intensely gloomy, has also become a complete catastrophe. The pursuit of truth was replaced by science with the pursuit of power. But now the power is so great that the World can easily be destroyed by explosion or pollution. The wonders of science turn into horrific Nazi-style experiments on the unborn. Science may be handy. As a philosophy of life it is dead.

I have already spoken of the failures of other religions. But their failures as ways of life must be emphasized. Christianity makes no impression on the real World, except to support injustice. The Christian left has died the same death as the left in general. Judaism still exists as a way of life, but in general is tied up with the deeds, misdeeds, and fate of Israel. Can anyone turn to Judaism as a way of life, in the knowledge that this will just make even more pathetic victims of the Palestinians?

The collapse of religion has resulted in the rise of a great variety of new cults, such as the Scientologists, Moonies, followers of Hare Krishna etc., etc. These cults are not the cure to the spiritual vacuum. They are rather symptoms of it. These cults in no way challenge the World of today. They preach a retreat into mysticism, and the building of Utopian communities of believers. The aim is total withdrawal from the World. The cults will never do more than feed off the helpless and defeated, who are driven to the edges and forced out of normal society. Their members are the utterly lost young, the rootless drifters in a society that has no place for the poor and alone. If you are totally lonely, these cults offer company. But the price is the most systematic exploitation of the young victims.

All over the World this failure of ideologies exists. In Latin America the Catholic Church is declining before the challenge of Protestant sects. In the Arab World Nasserites Socialism and Ba'athism are dead. In Indonesia Pancasila is a joke. In India the secularism of Nehru is finished, and the country returns to its sectarian roots. African Socialism of Nye ere is dead. Afro Communism of Samara Michel is equally dead. In this World of failure, Capitalism is succeeding, with its political brother, Capitalist Democracy. But the success of Capitalism is in fact a failure. The whole history of the last one hundred and fifty years has been the attempt to find an alternative to a money-centred, selfish, grubby, philistine and rotten society.

Now we are told that history has ended. From now on the system of systematic self-worship will rule. And everyone will be drawn into the pursuit of pleasure.

And the rich and the powerful will have their wishes blessed by regular victories in elections dominated by these same rich and powerful people through corrupt and corrupting television and newspapers. This success is the arrival of the Age of Ignorance itself, admiring itself in the mirror of its own hack journalists. This success of Capitalism is, of course, the cause in so many different ways, of the failure of the other beliefs.

Islam alone remains, and is advancing and succeeding all over the World. Islam earlier in this century experienced many problems. The reason was that people were deserting Islam in support of Science, or Capitalism, or Marxism. Now those people are returning, having seen the failure of those other beliefs. The advance of Islam is not a return to the Islam of yesterday. Rather it is a rediscovery of Islam, a going back to the fundamentals of Islam. That is why Islam is succeeding. The failure of all these ways of life leaves us with a basic need. We need a belief in the changeability of the World, and the making of it into a decent, kind place. As the failure of Marxism shows, and as the failure of Science also shows, this belief has to be God-based. And the only God-based belief in the changeability of the World is Islam.

Islam believes that God created man so that man should rule over God's creation in the place of God, and so be God's Vice-regent. God exists outside time and space, and so Man is to be a God-like being inside time and space. So a World can be created where Man can be this God-like creature. We must strive to change the World into a kind and decent place, fit for God's Vicegerent to live in. We can try to do this, knowing that God will support our every action, and finally bring us to Paradise. We can struggle without any fear of death, only with fear of God.

And if you are afraid of God, everyone is afraid of you. I am writing this book to appeal to the reader to consider Islam. One thing I must not forget to say is that all the best of their beliefs and ways of life come into Islam. Islam claims to complete religion. It builds on all that went before. So it inherits all the best that humanity has achieved.

Islam contains the intense social and political activism of Marxism. There is endless room for anyone who likes an active life. There is the love for the poor and oppressed that is central to the real Christianity. For Catholics, Mary the Mother of Jesus is an honoured person in Islam holding the highest place of any woman in Paradise. For Protestants there is the absence of priesthood, and the practical democracy of a belief with no Pope or hierarchy. There is the total monotheism of Judaism, and also the detailed religious lifestyle of Judaism, in Islam. For the Socialist there is the great love of ordinary people, and the hatred of any kind of snobbery. For the Anarchist there is the belief that Man has no master. In Islam you obey no man of any kind. But Islam is more anarchic than Anarchism, for the anarchist obeys one person, which is he. In Islam you obey only God, and not even yourself. Islam also possesses all the self-organisation of Syndicalism.

For the Conservative there is the Islamic love of age-old traditions. There is also the love of the family and trade. George Orwell wrote that the greatest feature of English life was the intense love of privacy. Islam manages to combine both sociability and privacy. Imam Ghazzali said that one of the signs of a person who loves God was that he liked to be alone. Private contemplation is the height of spirituality in Islam. The best Zikr (remembrance of God) is one done in private that is so quiet that even the Angels don't know that you are doing it. For those who love mysticism, Islam has Sufism. For the Buddhist Islam has its indifference to the World. The Muslim fears only God, and looks only to God. Nothing of this World can be of any importance at all.

Even for the frank Capitalist, Islam contains the best. Islam has private property, but no selfishness and a determination to clean away all the dirt and filth from riches. Islam hopes that the wealthy man will be the best man. Islam also has its moments for the philistine. There are the three Bids, which are marvellous celebrations at the end of Ramadan and the end of Hajj and on the birthday of the Prophet. There is the moral duty to engage in marital relations. There is the beautiful halal food. And also there are nice clothes: Man must be like God, and God is elegant.

Above all, Islam has all these marvellous features at once. All the best of these different beliefs you can choose to enjoy in Islam. But I cannot write a book on Islam without considering two subjects which are always used to abuse Islam. The first is the question of Islam and Women. The feminists charge Islam with oppressing women. And Islam is certainly not the same as feminism. The second is the question of the cutting off of hands as punishment for theft.

The question of Islam and feminism is too important a subject to be dealt with in one or two paragraphs, and I hope soon to write a book on it. My comments here are only brief. All agree that the life of women today is in great crisis. The difference between Islam and feminism is what to think about the crisis and what to do about it. Capitalism is destroying the life women used to lead all over the World. The family is ceasing to exist. The woman is drawn into the market place, as a labourer, and as a sexual commodity. Increasingly we live in a sex-obsessed society, where the aim is infinite sexual satisfaction. The woman gives up the family and children in return for money, as wage-labourer and prostitute. Feminism in general welcomes and supports this trend under Capitalism. To them the woman must welcome the end of the family, and seek to become a childless competitor, attempting to win the battle of Capitalism with men. To do these women must suppress all that is female in them. The aim is to be the wage-labourer and sexual commodity, but on better terms, "equal" terms.

Islam's attitude to the crisis is different. Woman is not well-equipped to fight the battle of Capitalism with men, and Women always have, and always will, lose the battle. The attempt to win the battle produces, alongside the death of God and the death of Man, the death of Woman, which may become a reality in the Twenty-First Century. The battle of Capitalism, also, is not worth winning. It is only organised self-worship. The aim for us all must rather be to be free of self, and to achieve the deepest spirituality and holiness, and perfect ourselves intellectually and morally.

For this reason, In Islam, Man is ordered by God to take care of Woman. The woman is not to have to earn her living. A man must support his female relatives. And a woman is shielded from all sexual exploitation. Islam prohibits any sexual cattle-market, such as we see in any dance-hall. The aim in Islam is sexual freedom for men and women. But this is not the positive freedom to engage in infinite sexual activity.

Such positive freedom is impossible to achieve, and is dangerous to attempt to achieve. In the process of attempting to achieve it people worship sexual desire and not God.

Sexual freedom in Islam is freedom from sexual desire, a life where sexual desire is under control at all the times, and never is put to any but good, God-given purposes. This negative freedom is achieved by universal marriage, so that no-one should ever burn. It is also achieved by the granting of complete sexual privacy, provided above all by Islamic dress, for both men and women. The aim is to lower our level of sexual excitement to the perfectly natural level. This negative freedom is not merely possible, but is easily achieved, and can be achieved by anyone, and is achieved by the huge mass of Muslims.

The feminists argue that the family is compulsory in modern society. This is nonsense. The family is extremely difficult to achieve in this society. Everything, from housing, to unemployment, to the cost of living, to the atomization of society, in reality forces us into loneliness and frustrated relationships. A huge mass of people in this society engage in no sexual activity of any kind. And how can anyone argue that the family is compulsory if one just thinks of the problems anyone encounters if they actually have a baby?

Islam is fighting to preserve the family in a society too selfish to allow it. The aim of Islam is to overcome the heartlessness of men. The Prophet (Peace and Blessings of Allah be upon Him) said that the best man was the one who was most kind to his wife and children. The Prophet (Peace and Blessings of Allah be upon Him) himself did the housework! Women must be free to become perfect and enter Paradise. Her private life in the home could, say the Prophet (Peace and Blessings of Allah be upon Him) be as spiritually rewarding as a man's life outside it. The aim for women is to enjoy the privilege of being shielded from the world by Man, so as to rise to be Vice-regent of God; along with Man. Woman is a complete equal of Man.

This is the spirit of Islam, and I feel that Islam can prevent the death of Woman. Just as the best of everything is in Islam, so the best of feminism is in Islam. Islam especially wishes to preserve female uniqueness and the female personality. Islam especially values the one achievement of women which is unique, which is children. And Islam has its own female separatism. It is known as Purdah. Needless to say, not all Muslims live up to these high standards for the life of women. Many Muslims engage in totally anti-Islamic practices, both eastern and western. In India there is big legacy of Hinduism in the treatment of women. In the west Islamic practices are often perverted in a totally Capitalist direction. The Muslims themselves betray the commands of Islam. But their failure to practice Islam in relation to women only resembles the failure in many other directions.

The practice of Islamic punishments for theft has also been cruelly distorted. Bankrupt regimes, keen to appear Islamic to please the masses they oppress, have cut off hands as the easiest and cheapest concession to Islam. This is totally to be condemned. The Islamic punishments are frightening. They are meant to be, for the criminal is defying the majesty of God. But the aim of Islam is a society totally free from crime. Islam agrees with the best criminology in teaching that it is society that prepares the crime. Islam aims to remove all causes of crime, so that a thief is really only defying almighty God if he steals.

In Islam theft is allowed to the absolutely poor. You may, indeed you must, steal to eat. In society there must not be any poverty. Zakat, the pillar of Islam, is the payment of a due to the poor. Unemployment is forbidden. But Islam goes much further. It removes all causes of crime. Any criminologist will tell you that the cause of most crime is failure to care for and control children. Children wandering out of control, commit the vast majority of crimes. Islam prevents this by its militant defence of the family. Most violent crime is committed due to alcohol. Islam prohibits alcohol totally. Islam's sexual code, which I have just detailed, eliminates the cause of sexual offences. An Islamic society is crime-free. Historically Muslim societies were well known for the absence of crime. It was the Europeans, and colonialism, which destroyed the family, introduced alcohol, fostered prostitution etc.

Thus one can say that the Islamic punishments would be rarely or never applied. There would be no cause for crime, or if there was a cause for crime there would be no cause for punishment. The complete bankruptcy of western penal systems needs no comment. The penalties in the past were far more severe than the Islamic penalties. In the Middle Ages one was executed in England for stealing five pence or more. The penalties were relaxed, but due to the huge wave of criminality, now totally out of control, which meant, and means, that no prison could ever be big enough to hold all the criminals. Today the West is going back to a savagery that has no justification in the Law of God, and will be applied in complete disregard of the way Capitalism prepares the crimes.

All the ways of running human affairs have failed in the Twentieth Century, leaving only the systematic selfishness of Capitalism, or Islam. I can never accept the systematic worship of the self.

That is the reason why, for me, Islam alone remains.

VI The Truth of Islam

My final reason for becoming a Muslim has been the truth of Islam. I feel Islam is something I can completely believe in and accept as true. This is the most difficult of all my reasons to actually prove. One can offer all manner of evidence, and arguments, but the difficulty of proof always remains. However that difficulty is itself strictly in accordance with Islam's fundamental principles.

The aim of God in creating the World was to produce, in time and space, a being resembling God, able to rule the World in God's place. That person must resemble God above all in the commitment to goodness and decency. Now that goodness and decency would be most genuine, indeed could only be genuine, if achieved with no absolute guarantee of either punishment or reward. Those people who could rise to the stature of God without relying on certainty really would resemble God. They would be kind and decent, despite the seeming absence of any rewards and punishments. If man only wished to resemble God out of fear or desire for favour, he could never resemble God. So there can never be certainty for the human being. Islam stresses that what you believe in is the unseen. You will never be given complete proof or certainty in this life. If you have belief, it is from God alone. And that belief can never be certain completely.

In a very important sense, Islam relies on the philosophical primacy of good deeds. The Muslim is the person who is determined to lead the kindest, most generous life, who is determined to lift up the oppressed, the poor and the downtrodden, and change the World into a fit place for mankind. The Muslim is the person who seeks for the philosophy of life which will enable him to do just that. That philosophy comes first which most promotes good deeds. That philosophy has to be the belief in a merciful and compassionate God who created Man so that Man could build Paradise. In the Quran you always find good deeds linked with belief. Good deeds build belief. Good deeds lead me to the philosophy of Islam. If I do a selfless act of kindness, with no benefit to me in this World, and even danger, even mortal danger, am I not saying that a God exists who will make my act genuinely successful even if I have to wait until the end of time. My deeds show what my belief really is. My deeds show what my belief must be. My deeds always speak louder than my words. My deeds speak louder even than my private thoughts. Good deeds are a true act of faith, and are faith itself.

Islam is saying: go ahead and do good deeds, and have faith that this is not in vain. I feel I am able to accept that. I can accept the philosophical primacy of good deeds. I can accept that a good person, who fails, only appears to fail, and only appears to fail in the eyes of fools. The truly wise, the truly philosophical will always know that, though the good person dies, yet he still lives. I cannot accept Marxism. The analysis of society and history is brilliant. The morality is so fine.

But in the end, the rejection of life after death destroys the Marxist. The philosophy cannot put goodness first. Ultimately the Marxist must say: if I am defeated, then all is lost. The philosophical primacy of good deeds destroys Marxism. A Marxist may press on Regardless with good deeds. In which case he is accepting Islam in deeds, and Marxist philosophy in words, and thoughts. I know that I myself was doing that at earlier times of my life. Most other beliefs don't even try to be good. They accept philosophies which put oppression and bad deeds in first place.

Islam is thus implicit in the wish to do good deeds. All who wish to be good are searching for Islam. And remember that Islam says that the search for good deeds has to be in the dark. A good deed must always involve an act of faith. You will always have to make a philosophical assumption when you the truth of Islam will always be faith and not certainty. Of course, the whole point about philosophy is its uncertainty. Philosophy is the science of Unanswerable questions. The opponents of Islam can never know for certain that Islam is false. But we must recollect What Hazrat Ali (May Allah be pleased with him) said: if He Muslim is wrong, he has lived a marvellous life. While the non-believer has lived a dreadful life. If the Muslim is Right, he really gets Paradise, while the evil man gets hell.

The uncertainty of philosophy has been made to play a philosophical role by the ideologists of Capitalism. If we cannot know the truth, then all we can ever be justified in doing, they say, is letting us each go his own way. So uncertainty here leads to the right of selfishness. You cannot dare to restrict my freedom on any philosophical grounds! But Islam also is based on the uncertainty of philosophy. Nothing can be proved. Any religion or atheism that pretends to proof is simply wrong. But Islam arrives at decency and good deeds from this philosophical uncertainty. Man can never have any definite reason not to be his most noble, and to lead the best moral life. Man, in his uncertainty, cannot dare to do anything else. But if, in his uncertainty, he does the most noble deeds, what a truly wonderful being Man is, and how fitting a Vice-regent of God.

God could clearly never fulfil such an aim unless philosophy was uncertain. The last step to Islam must be an act of faith. I have given six reasons why I accepted Islam. Now I can pick out the key reason. I really believe Islam because of its morality. Islam is true for me because it believes in goodness, kindness and decency, because it has the highest morality. I believe that in this world, also, Islam alone remains able to foster the life of goodness and decency. But I also believe that the only way to come to Islam is to value goodness and decency. God alone gives faith. To me the way to faith is to lead the life Islam commands.

This means, of course, engaging in the practices of the Prophet, praying, fasting and all the other practices of Islam, and also training you to do good deeds. Imam Ghazzali wrote that this was the proof of Islam. For if you led this life, finally you would feel the Breeze of Paradise blowing inside you. Then you would go beyond faith, to knowledge and to proof. We should note carefully exactly what Imam Ghazzali wrote. The proof of Islam is the overpowering joy of goodness and decency. Helping the oppressed and downtrodden, changing the World into a decent and kind place, results in an overpowering ecstasy. You choose this path because of the desire to do good deeds.

When this experience of ecstasy arrives, then you know that there can only be one solution to the problem of philosophical uncertainty.

That is the reason why I believe in the truth of Islam.

Conclusion

Now that I have given my reasons for becoming a Muslim, I should by way of conclusion perhaps talk of my life since becoming a Muslim, and that means of my joys, regrets and hopes. My main joy has been an end to fear. In atheism there is, inevitably, a fear of the finality of death, and the pointlessness of life, and a fear of the triumph of the oppressor, and the absence of justice from life. Islam banishes this completely. Islam teaches you to fear only God. It has also taught me to feel sorry for the wicked, for they face a truly terrible future.

Many religions bring as many fears as they remove. They are full of superstitions, and the god they worship is savage. Islam, on the contrary, is devoid of superstitions. The Prophet (Peace and Blessings of Allah be upon Him) is a very real historical figure, and no-one is required to believe anything on the basis of anything other than sound historical scholarship. The belief in the oneness of God in Islam also banishes superstition. There are no saints and minor gods. Fortune telling is forbidden to Muslims. Only God knows the future. God is merciful and full of love for the mankind. While you should fear God, the Quran also says that God is absolutely just, and we must never think that anything God will do is unreasonable or oppressive in any way. God is more just than Man can ever be. We should never attribute any abomination to God. We must look in any aspect of Islam for the love and kindness, and never accept interpretation of any Islamic Law in an oppressive way.

Islam banishes all fears. The Islamic life of prayer, five times a day, and fasting etc is a marvellous thing. The aim of Islam is to uplift the downtrodden and oppressed. To do this you must carry out the law God has laid down for human life. But the great danger is that, having discovered the law of life, you might forget it. In Marxism it is clear that the ideas of Marx were forgotten, and covered with rust, and that was one major reason for Marxism's failure. But saying prayers five times a day, and engaging in the other practices, such as regular fasting, stops you forgetting the basic ideas. You are constantly returned to thinking of God, and the Prophet (Peace and Blessings of Allah be upon Him).

Another of my joys is the feeling of there being a real purpose in helping the oppressed. Oppression truly ends when the oppressed person leads a morally good life. Oppression is wrong because it destroys the oppressed morally and spiritually. The fault with many Liberation movements is that they free people from one oppression, only to transfer them to another. Poverty ends, for example, but only to give way to life of drunkenness. The oppressed are freed, but then acquire the attitudes of the oppressor. The poor white goes to a life of wealth in Africa, only to impose a dreadful life on the black people there. The Jews leave persecution in Europe to impose persecution on the Palestinians.

But Islam, in freeing the oppressed, directs them to the life of goodness. That is vital. In Islam the oppressed can advance to a truly wonderful life, full of dignity and kindness. Islam is thus the true liberation. The poor, ignorant, and persecuted will know real wealth, knowledge and equality if they come to Islam. Islam truly is, for this reason, the path to real freedom.

My regrets are many. It is difficult to talk to people about Islam because of the racism surrounding it. It is difficult to get a hearing because of the screaming of the anti-Islamic media. Almost no-one ever sees a truly positive picture of Islam presented. But of course, that is what one would expect. The people who shout against Islam are themselves oppressors. It is the proof of the goodness of Islam that such people hate it. If it was oppressive, they would love it. These same people love inequality, racism, ignorance and superstition.

But my major regret is that the Muslims themselves are not Muslims enough. When I visit Muslim families, their children are often behaving in a non-Muslim way, running after a lot of silliness. Many Muslim leaders apologise for Islam, and try to toady to the oppressor. The oppressor, of course, will never accept these creeps as equal. Above all, the Muslims divide into sects. Sectarianism is totally foreign to Islam. And one must not exaggerate its importance. For example, there are about fifteen Mosques in the town I live in, and I can pray in every one on any day. This could not be said for one second about Christianity. For them it is an enormous breakthrough even to visit each others' churches, never mind to share an act of worship. But there is division after division in the Muslim Community. I reject all of this. There is only one God, one Quran, and one Kabah. I regard myself as just a Muslim, and no more.

All has gone well since I became a Muslim. When I became a Muslim, at the actual ceremony, a man told me that he had been born a Muslim. He said that, while I was beginning to learn about Islam, he was still learning new things after forty years. My hope is to really go more deeply into Islam and taste its joys more deeply. I also hope to understand better the way Islam answers life's problems. But I really hope and pray that the Islamic movement will grow and develop, and bring real hope and relief to the oppressed. As an Englishman, I pray for the conversion of England. But I also pray that those who read this book, even if they cannot accept Islam, will view Islam in a more kindly light, and see Islam as an immensely valuable contribution to the life of humanity.

Finally I pray that those who read this book will remember God. In the remembrance of Allah do human hearts find satisfaction.

Alhamdulillah!
Dr Muhammad Haroon

.